Canoeing Up C

Other Books by Philip Whalen

The Calendar

Decompressions: Selected Poems

The Diamond Noodle

The Education Continues Along
Including Voyages: A TransPacific Journal

Enough Said: Fluctuat Nec Mergitur: Poems 1974–1979

Every Day: Poems

Heavy Breathing: Poems 1967–1980

Highgrade: Doodles, Poems

Imaginary Speeches for a Brazen Head, a Novel

The Invention of the Letter: A Beastly Morality {Being an
Illuminated Moral History, for the Edification of Younger
Readers}

The Kindness of Strangers: Poems 1969–1974

Like I Say: Poems

Memoirs of an Interglacial Age

Monday, in the Evening, 21:VIII:61

Off the Wall: Interviews with Philip Whalen

On Bear's Head

On Bread & Poetry: A Panel Discussion with Gary Snyder,
Lew Welch & Philip Whalen

Prolegomena to a Study of the Universe

Severance Pay: Poems, 1967–1969

Scenes of Life at the Capital

Three Satires

T/O

You Didn't Even Try

Canoeing Up Cabarga Creek

BUDDHIST POEMS
1955-1986

Philip Whalen

Selected and Arranged
by Miriam Sagan and Robert Winson

Parallax Press
Berkeley, California

"Epigrams & Imitations" appeared in Pinchpenny 1985.
Most of the poems in this book have been previously published by
Grey Fox Press and the Four Seasons Foundation, San Francisco.
Permission from the publisher, Donald Allen, is gratefully
acknowledged.

Parallax Press
P.O. Box 7355
Berkeley, California 94707

Drawings by the Author.
Cover photograph by Dan Howe.
Author photograph by Barbara Lubanski Wenger.
Design by Legacy Media, Inc.

Printed in the United States of America.

Library of Congress Cataloging-In-Publication Data
Whalen, Philip.
    Canoeing Up Cabarga Creek : Buddhist poems 1955–1986/
by Philip Whalen.
        p. cm.
    ISBN 0-938077-79-1 (pbk.)
    1. Buddhist poetry, American   I. Title.
PS3545.H117C36   1996
811'.54—dc20   96-11499
                                                    CIP

Dedicated to the memory of
Robert Sycamore Winson,
Seigen Yōsan, SkyCourse WillowMountain

Contents

Foreword
by Allen Ginsberg

The interesting history of Philip Whalen: he encountered William Carlos Williams at Reed College with Gary Snyder and Lew Welch; also Pound, Chinese influences, etc., 1950...Snyder said (1955), "Better poet than myself"...Ted Berrigan and/or Ed Sanders: "Imitate everything Philip Whalen does"... Buddhism was belittled 1956 as "fad", "Beat Zen etc.", but "nothing promised that was not performed:" Philip Whalen, Roshi, now is First "Beat" or "San Francisco Renaissance" Poet Zen teacher...Shy, grumpy, endearing, Abbot of Hartford Street Zen Center, San Francisco, Zen lineage of Shunryu Suzuki Roshi.

An elder age 72 as of this volume, here's an anthology of overtly dharmic works out of the larger mass of his verse— a unique presentation of a master poet in American language writing new Zen poetry with the discipline of open form, notational spontaneity. An object lesson to academic sour- pusses who've disapproved the mode—here rigorous train- ing in free mind itself supersedes the imitative superficial "discipline" of outworn metrical stanzaic spoken forms. The latter are appropriate for stringed lyric, but not for medita- tive practice of "writing the mind".

As Jack Kerouac's poetry was praised by Chögyam Trungpa, Rinpoche, for its open form as "a perfect manifes- tation of mind," so Whalen wrote, following same principles 1959, "This poetry is a picture or graph of the mind moving."

From "Unfinished, 3:XII:55" we have a prophetically di- dactic poem, as if a teacher's instructions. "Sourdough Moun- tain Lookout", is an early matrix for a venerable tradition of the poet working in Forest Service as summer fire lookout (as Snyder worked, as did Kerouac inspired by this "Sourdough" poem, with resultant novels *Dharma Bums* and *Desolation Angels*). This poem in its historic place was chef d'oeuvre along with "Howl" and Snyder's "Berry Feast" at celebrated Six Gallery poetry reading inaugurating San Francisco Poetry Renaissance's 1955 cycle; printed in Robert Creeley's final Black Mountain Review #7, reprinted in ground-breaking Donald Allen *New American Poetry Anthology* 1960, much reprinted since. A montage of casual conscious moments, awakened mind-flashes mixed with apposite quotes from 4th century Chinese brush masters, old trail crew farts, Heraclitus, Dr. Johnson, Empedocles, Buddha, ending with the first recorded "hip" translation of Prajñaparamita Mantra adapted from Gary Snyder version. Altogether a modern U.S. dharmic ideogram statement that's survived, still memorable after four decades.

"Hymnus Ad Patrem Sinensis" shows characteristic swift wit, re scroll brushwork "on paper held together now by little more than ink...", and characteristic beat-style word slinging:... "conked out among the busted spring rain cherry-blossom winejars"...

"Haiku, for Gary Snyder" captures the abrupt movement of a dragonfly, & signifies emptiness: "Here's a dragonfly/... Where it was,/that place no longer exists."

"A Vision of the Bodhisattvas": How'd he decide to be a living Buddha? "What am I waiting for?/A change in customs that will take 1000 years to come about?" So that "I can't help feeling this world is immortality:" ("Philippic, against White-head and a Friend".)

What's that world look like?: "Clear white ice moon sparkle," ("Winter Jelly.") And to prove it, a tipsy appreciation of Kyoto's millennial charms, her river same as his boyhood Oregon's White River ("White River Ode.")

He's excellent at moment snapshots, in imagistic tradition, with his own associative spin as: "Above the Shrine." And a curious political angle, radical libertarian, calm and grounded, from "The War Poem for Diane di Prima": "All I wanted was something translated by R. H. Blyth,/18,000 pounds of napalm and a helicopter,/Why do I keep losing the war? Misplacing it?"

His conclusion? agreeing with Diane di Prima's "Rant" (*Pieces of a Song: Selected Poems,* City Lights, San Francisco, 1990); "The war is only temporary, the revolution is/Immediate change in vision/Only imagination can make it work." His Bodhisattva vow: "I'll return to America one of these days/I refuse to leave it to slobs and boobies/I'll have it all back, I won't let it go." And the so-called national war? As of 1966, three decades before official Vietnam War-Lord McNamara's formal repentance: "Nobody wants the war only the money/fights on, alone." ("The War Poem for Diane di Prima")

His "Grace Before Meat" is a homemade classic, the adaptation of a traditional awareness reminder at table. "Kitchen Practice", a taste of tolerant exasperation, himself later to be head monk at Tassajara Zen Mountain Center. "Zenshinji," "Somebody Else's Problem," & "Back to Normalcy" display nuts & bolts inside the maturing teacher's head. From late '70s on, poems glimpse particular moments, thoughts, vagaries, of an enlightened unenlightened monk. From "The Ghosts": "A new ghost in this morning's dream,/Beautiful and young and still alive/How far will that one follow me? I'm not chasing any,/Any more."

So nothing promised that was not performed: from "What Are You Studying, These Days?": "I have put on a gown of power I didn't know I had—/Or wanted."

Allen Ginsberg
New York 4/24/95

Introduction
by Zentatsu Richard Baker-rōshi

Philip Whalen, Zenshin Ryūfū, is my teacher, and I am his teacher. We have shared these roles. I first met Philip in 1959 with Michael McClure at Grove Press in New York. They were there for poetry readings. I was an employee of Grove. I remember Philip's warm and blustery presence in the office halls. He moved as if he didn't entirely want to be where he was, and yet it felt that he knew exactly where he was. I liked his feeling and presence. We only exchanged a few words.

When I moved to San Francisco in the Fall of 1960, I was searching for Zen and for a language. I had already discovered the language of Philip, Michael McClure, Ezra Pound, Allen Ginsberg, Gary Snyder, Robert Duncan, and Charles Olsen. All of them helped bring me into Buddhism. I intuitively knew I had to free my language (and my concepts of life and relationships) from the East Coast—from New York and Boston. Coming to San Francisco, I did not expect to meet Philip again, or to meet Gary or Robert, who also became important in my life. That was far from my mind. In NYC you didn't meet people just because you lived there. For me, reading them was enough. However, the day I arrived in San Francisco, I ran into a friend, Don Allen, who had been the Grove Press and *Evergreen Review* editor. He told me he had recently seen Philip. I remember saying, "His language is on my mind more than that of any other poet."

Philip's language has a life of its own. It often jumps off the page, separating itself from the poem into an objective existence. Sometimes it is in caps. Sometimes, handwritten in his vivid calligraphy. Suddenly, there may be words and letters somewhere between the reader and the page, carrying us into a tangible world of the poem. The poem is now in front of us, in our hands. His poems are more objects than mental impressions stuck to the page.

Philip's poems often abruptly change voice or location through inflection or content. They move into our location, our location while we are reading. Or the poem may bump us into locations from the past, or into places we don't recognize—but Philip seems clear about. Then the poem, when it works for us, brings resolution, or a sigh about a lack of resolution. ("Some day I guess I'll never learn"; "Stop writing it down"; "This doesn't explain anything"; "what'll you be like in your prime?"; "Shall I drop my gold crown in the pool?")

Philip's poetry was liberating and contributed to my entry into practice. Before I came to California, I read his poem, "A Vision of the Bodhisattvas":

They pass before me one by one riding on animals
"What are you waiting for," they want to know

Z—, young as he is (& mad into the bargain) tells me
"Some day you'll drop everything & become
         a *rishi*, you know."

I know
The forest is there, I've lived in it
         more certainly than this town? Irrelevant—

         What am I waiting for?
A change in customs that
         will take 1000 years to come about?
Who's to make the change but me?

                  "Returning again and again," Amida says

Why's that dream so necessary? walking out
    of whatever house alone
Nothing but the clothes on my back, money or no
Down the road to the next place
    the highway leading to the mountains
From which I absolutely must come back

What business have I to do that?
I know the world and I love it too much and it
Is not the one I'd find outside this door.

I was reading koans. About a thousand years had passed
since most of the principals had lived. I asked myself, along
with Philip, "What am I waiting for? A change in customs
that will take 1000 years to come about? Who's to make the
change but me?" The men and women of those koans hadn't
waited, why should I?

And I knew the "forest" he meant. I also loved the world—
including the one I found outside my door where Bodhisattvas were riding by. I followed them to San Francisco.
Then meeting Suzuki-rōshi, I began to practice.

Of course, I did not know at the time that this poem was
a prediction that Philip would become a Rōshi and that I
would be part of that prediction. (Perchance, our Buddhist
names both start with "Z.")

I also praised (as he did in 1958), "those ancient China-
men/ Who left me a few words...A line of poetry...on paper
held together now by little more than ink/& their own
strength brushed momentarily over it". In '58 I was in the
Merchant Marine sailing to India reading Ezra Pound and
Arthur Waley, getting to know those ancient Chinamen who
were saving me and who surely would have been, as Philip
writes, "Happy to have saved us all."

When I first arrived in San Francisco, I met Philip occasionally, but mostly I admired him from a distance. Then I found we were both moving to Japan about the same time. Our friend Gary Snyder had already been living in Japan for twelve years. When he moved to the States in 1968 with Masa and Kai, his new baby, he invited us—Virginia, baby daughter Sally, and myself—to take his beautiful traditional Japanese house and garden. In the process of moving, our two families lived in the house together in Kyōto for a few weeks. Phil came to Japan a bit later, in early 1969, and at first lived with us in our new house from Gary. Then he moved to a tiny six mat room near Antaiji on the hill above us, and then to Gunther Nietschke's house in Fukuōji-chō near Ninnaji. He was living in Japan for the second time, and I and my family for the first time.

Philip lived as he wrote in "Since You Ask Me":

My life has been spent in the midst of heroic landscapes
which never overwhelmed me and yet I live in a single
room in the city—the room a lens focusing on a sheet
of paper. Or the inside of your head.
How do you like your world?

In Japan Phil came over and meditated with us once, but this is not the relationship we had then. Phil knew the secrets and the lore of many temples and mostly we went to temples together. We took day excursions. And occasionally longer trips—to Mount Kōya and Eiheiji. We would roam about, complaining of the obfuscating customs, of the muggy heat or the cold, and loving every moment of it—the extraordinariness of everything and our great good fortune in being there. Usually we would end up in a restaurant—and often a new one Phil had heard about or had been to during his first time in Japan. We had a very good time—sometimes to the amusement of the other patrons for we never got it all quite right.

It was in America when I was abbot of the San Francisco Zen Center, that we started to practice together formally. I was relieved to have Phil as a companion on the way. Our intermingling paths and his understanding—already present in his poems—made it clear to me that I would give him transmission one day. He was already one of the American Zen pioneers having done a first experimental sesshin in a cabin in Mill Valley sometime in 1955 or '56, with Albert Saijo, Gary, and a few others. It was Albert, Phil says, who taught them about cushions, a schedule, how to sit, kinhin (walking meditation between sitting periods), Zen eating, and tea ceremony. Albert had been a student of Nyogen Senzaki.

Philip practiced in San Francisco at first and then began to go to Tassajara for Practice Periods. A time he describes as "a life of elegant retirement in the character of a Zen Buddhist priest at the Hossen Temple in San Francisco and at the monastery of Zenshinji at Tassajara Springs, far in the mountains east of Big Sur." His first ninety-day Practice Period at Tassajara was the fall of '72. Altogether, he did ten Practice Periods and one summer at Tassajara. His last was the fall of '82. In 1981 and the first half of '82 Phil headed a small center on Fairmont Street in order to try out creating a neighborhood practice center in a part of the city that was a ways from the Page Street main Zendō.

Then from 1984 through '87, at our Santa Fe Zen Center on Cerro Gordo Road, we practiced and studied together every day. During this time we completed the Transmission studies. Zenshin Ryūfū (Zen Heart, Dragon Wind), Philip Whalen, truly entered the Mind of the Dongshan lineage and of Suzuki-rōshi. On July, 1987, at Crestone Mountain Zen Center, we did the formal ceremonies and empowerments. Zenshin Ryūfū is my first fully transmitted student in Suzuki-rōshi's lineage. It was also the first Transmission Ceremony done at the Crestone Monastery and thus a consecration of the monastery. ("Transmission" means to receive and realize the Mind, spirit, and essential teachings of your teacher and lineage. When the title "Rōshi" is given, it means this realization has matured and flowered in practice.)

During 1979–80 at Tassajara, as part of preparation for Transmission, I asked Zenshin to keep an off-and-on journal of daily poems. He called the journal, "Watch the Lion Turning." On the early pages he wrote:

Change the outside, build a
    fire in the stove
Change the inside with
    chicken flavoured bouillon

"Poetry is a destructive force"
        —headline from Wallace
        Stevens

"Nothing about me
        gonna be the same"
        —threat from an
            old song

So many people want me to say
"Poetry & Buddhism are
mutually exclusive"

Po Chü-I apologized for being
"Enthralled by the Daemon of
            Poesie"
{I think he meant that he
was sorry not to have become
a Buddhist monk}

Buddhism destroys illusions of
    destruction & construction &

Vanishes away
    like chicken soup.

"Strike through the mask"
    Mr. Melville says.
The Tendai people said

    TSUI MIN

"RENEWED DESTRUCTION"
          {Bruno Petzold, p.324}

        TON
        GO
        MYŌ
        SHŪ

"sudden enlightenment;
wonderful practice"

    Leave town.

"Watch the Lion Turning" was not meant to be published,
but here are a few of his entries:

Sun's out of business
Clouds go on shining
Not a minute to lose

———————————————

"Not to wear jewels,
Long hair, shiny clothes"
How can I be Kwannon
    any more?

———————————

Having been wicked in youth
I can be an innocent old man
    (—don't get too close.)

———————————

The world all stuck together
        wet dead leaves
Nothing can be done quickly
The fire wants to be rebuilt
        twice in a row
The cat alleges that she's abused,
        forgotten, misunderstood
My rope belt ties itself into
        magic spontaneous knots
Doesn't want to work this morning

I plod and bungle as if I were
        The Government of the United
States

———————————

Whatever else right or wrong
I made the dog & the goldfish
    happy
        today
           {I think}

———————————

        Hard to say—
Is this the last of the old
Or the first outpost of the new
Timeless won't tell

And being right isn't enough

Comrade Lenin
Comrade Jesus
Comrade Einstein
_____

Put away books
        extra lamps
            table
Sit like I used to do
        (1946)
Turn away from sound,
        light, sense

To search
            a thought like a
                floodlight
            in a prison yard

    no escape
_____

I have peopled the world
with imperfect
            inferior beings
How could I have made
            such a mistake?
_____

    If you gave me the universe
            in a spoon
I might look at it a minute
Before I went back to my
                own
Where spoons & universes
        have no meaning

When I'm awake I don't move.
When I'm asleep I imagine
That I'm sitting still:

*

HOWSOMEVER,

YOU SCRUFFY ANTIQUE BUD =
DHAS,
TAKE THIS RAIN AWAY!

*

Out in the pasture
Wearing fur & horns
How can the buffalo
Become Kuei Shan?

What is Cabarga Creek? It is a creek at Tassajara that has no water—except during the spring runoff. From the Tassajara River it goes up under the bridge, up past Philip's usual cabin, past the shop and washing area, past the gate, and up the mountain to some damp spring. Sometimes it rushes. As Philip's muse. It had been a creek without a name, unrecognized, unnegotiable, usually dry, small. It got its name when Tassajara was nearly flooded with water from the immense runoff after the forest fire of 1977 and this no-name creek was raging under the bridge. If I remember correctly, I said, "Now it deserves a name, let's call it Cabarga Creek after Tom Cabarga." Tom said, "Nothing has ever been named for me before."

In "Warnings, Responses, Etc." Phil writes:

a mountain creek under logs over boulders
potholes in its bed patches of gravel the water
invariably falls into eddies at particular points breaks
into spray or spreads in heavy darkness as long as the
     water
source high up the canyon no end in sight
     beyond vinemaple
overhang downstream

flows

        & & & & & & & &

Cabarga Creek is also Philip's difficult muse. Often out to
lunch. Late! Preoccupied with someone else. But with Phil's
genius—the world, poetry, his muse cannot stay away long.
He will put the canoe right down on the rocks and start row-
ing upstream toward the source, "To hunt for words under
the stones/Blessing the demons that they may be freed" ("The
Bay Trees Were About to Bloom"). Magically water appears.
    He begins "Plums, Metaphysics, an Investigation, a Visit,
and a Short Funeral Ode":

           O Muse!
I don't dare summon you
All I ask is that I might come to you
Only to see you, only to look
      at your face
If you're too mad or too busy for a talk
      I'll go home soon.

            *

Smog this morning
Hot soupy sun
The mailman brought all the wrong letters
The air stinks, the birds are in somebody else's yard
Boys left a yellow broom in the plum tree
            (the plums are still green, however fat)
I hear the Scavengers' Protective Association complaining
            about the garbage cans, I

            worry about the fragility of my verses
            their failure to sound fresh and new

By God, here's the garbage men stealing green plums!

The water surfaces in the smallest instances. In a poem,
I don't know where I read it—I think it's a note poem
of some kind to Ron Loewinsohn—the alphabet surfaces,
"abcdefghijklmnopqrstuvwxyz." I read the alphabet again
slowly. It's like stone steps to a Buddhist temple.

I hope this book introduces many to Philip's poems and
opens up his other poems—often implicitly Buddhist—that
are not here. Indulge yourself in his informed intelligence,
his whimsy and wisdom.

Thank you, Philip, Zenshin Ryūfū Rōshi, for letting me
write this introduction to *Canoeing Up Cabarga Creek* because it caused me to read all these poems again.

We have both followed "down the road to the next place
the highway leading to the mountains". But as Philip said, "I
absolutely must come back"—to the world outside the door,
to help others, to help oneself, to practice with others.

His door now is the Hartford Street Zendō, where he is
abbot, succeeding Issan Dorsey Rōshi. Until 1993, the next-
door, "Maitri," a hospice for people with AIDS, was run by
the Zendō and friends.

In "Minor Moralia," 1959–1962, part 1:

"FEED THE HUNGRY. HEAL THE SICK.
    RAISE THE DEAD."

there's precious little else to do

What else do you know, what else?
Oh yes.
After you understand it all
How do you behave?

Let me end with Phil's poem, "Secret":

The great secret books are available to all. There are
copies in most libraries; they can be bought in cheap
paper editions. However accessible, they are still secret
books. The careless, the casual, the thoughtless reader
will come away from them no wiser than he was before.
The really secret books are dictated to me by my own ears
and I write down what they say.

I still ask with Zenshin Whalen-rōshi, that "Vision of the
Bodhisattvas...Returning again and again...Why's that dream
so necessary?"

Zentatsu Richard Baker
Crestone, Colorado October 12, 1995

Canoeing Up Cabarga Creek

BUDDHIST POEMS
1955–1986

Unfinished, 3:XII:55

We have so much
That contemplating it
We never learn the use—

Poisoning ourselves with food, with books
    with sleep

Ignorance quicker than cyanide
Cuts us down

No lack of opportunity to learn;
Flat-footed refusal! Call it
Perversion, abuse, bullheadedness
It is rejection of all we know

A single waking moment destroys us
And we cannot live without
Ourselves

You come to me for an answer? I
Invented it all, I
Am your tormentor, there is no
Escape, no redress

You are powerless against me: You
Must suffer agonies until you know
You are suffering;

Work on that.

BODHISATTVA IN BEAR WORLD

Sourdough Mountain Lookout

for Kenneth Rexroth

Tsung Ping (375–443): "Now I am old and infirm. I fear I shall no more
be able to roam among the beautiful mountains. Clarifying my mind, I
meditate on the mountain trails and wander about only in dreams."—in
The Spirit of the Brush, translated by Shio Sakanishi, page 34.

I always say I won't go back to the mountains
I am too old and fat there are bugs mean mules
And pancakes every morning of the world

Mr. Edward Wyman (63)
Steams along the trail ahead of us all
Moaning, "My poor old feet ache, my back
Is tired and I've got a stiff prick"
Uprooting alder shoots in the rain

Then I'm alone in a glass house on a ridge
Encircled by chiming mountains
With one sun roaring through the house all day
& the others crashing through the glass all night
Conscious even while sleeping

  Morning fog in the southern gorge
  Gleaming foam restoring the old sea-level
  The lakes in two lights green soap and indigo
  The high cirque-lake black half-open eye

Ptarmigan hunt for bugs in the snow
Bear peers through the wall at noon
Deer crowd up to see the lamp
A mouse nearly drowns in the honey

I see my bootprints mingle with deer-foot
Bear-paw mule-shoe in the dusty path to the privy

Much later I write down:
     "raging. Viking sunrise
     The gorgeous death of summer in the east"
(Influence of a Byronic landscape—
Bent pages exhibiting depravity of style.)

Outside the lookout I lay nude on the granite
Mountain hot September sun but inside my head
Calm dark night with all the other stars

HERACLITUS: "The waking have one common world
But the sleeping turn aside
Each into a world of his own."

I keep telling myself what I really like
Are music, books, certain land and sea-scapes
The way light falls across them, diffusion of
Light through agate, light itself...I suppose
I'm still afraid of the dark

          "Remember smart-guy there's something
          Bigger something smarter than you."
          Ireland's fear of unknown holies drives
          My father's voice (a country neither he
          Nor his great-grandfather ever saw)

          A sparkly tomb a plated grave
          A holy thumb beneath a wave

Everything else they hauled across Atlantic
Scattered and lost in the buffalo plains

Among these trees and mountains
From Duns Scotus to this page
A thousand years

       ("... a dog walking on his hind legs—
       not that he does it well but that he
       does it at all.")

Virtually a blank except for the hypothesis
That there is more to a man
Than the contents of his jock-strap

EMPEDOCLES: "At one time all the limbs
Which are the body's portion are brought together
By Love in blooming life's high season; at another
Severed by cruel Strife, they wander each alone
By the breakers of life's sea."

Fire and pressure from the sun bear down
Bear down centipede shadow of palm-frond
A limestone lithograph—oysters and clams of stone
Half a black rock bomb displaying brilliant crystals
Fire and pressure Love and Strife bear down
Brontosaurus, look away

My sweat runs down the rock

HERACLITUS: "The transformations of fire
are, first of all, sea; and half of the sea
is earth, half whirlwind....
It scatters and it gathers; it advances
and retires."

I move out of a sweaty pool

(The sea!)
And sit up higher on the rock

Is anything burning?

The sun itself! Dying

Pooping out, exhausted
Having produced brontosaurus, Heraclitus
This rock, me,
To no purpose
I tell you anyway (as a kind of loving)...
Flies & other insects come from miles around
To listen
I also address the rock, the heather,
The alpine fir

BUDDHA: "All the constituents of being are
Transitory: Work out your salvation with diligence."

(And everything, as one eminent disciple of that master
Pointed out, has been tediously complex ever since.)

There was a bird
Lived in an egg
And by ingenious chemistry
Wrought molecules of albumen
To beak and eye
Gizzard and craw
Feather and claw

My grandmother said:
"Look at them poor bed-
raggled pigeons!"

And the sign in McAlister Street:

> "IF YOU CAN'T COME IN
> SMILE AS YOU GO BY
> L♡VE
> THE BUTCHER

I destroy myself, the universe (an egg)
And time—to get an answer:
There are a smiler, a sleeper and a dancer

We repeat our conversation in the glittering dark
Floating beside the sleeper.
The child remarks, "You knew it all the time."
I: "I keep forgetting that the smiler is
Sleeping; the sleeper, dancing."

From Sauk Lookout two years before
Some of the view was down the Skagit
To Puget Sound: From above the lower ranges,
Deep in forest—lighthouses on clear nights.

This year's rock is a spur from the main range
Cuts the valley in two and is broken
By the river; Ross Dam repairs the break,
Makes trolley buses run
Through the streets of dim Seattle far away.

I'm surrounded by mountains here
A circle of 108 beads, originally seeds
         of *ficus religiosa*
               Bo-Tree
A circle, continuous, one odd bead
Larger than the rest and bearing

A tassel (hair-tuft) (the man who sat
          under the tree)
In the center of the circle,
A void, an empty figure containing
All that's multiplied;
Each bead a repetition, a world
Of ignorance and sleep.

Today is the day the goose gets cooked
Day of liberation for the crumbling flower
Knobcone pinecone in the flames
Brandy in the sun

Which, as I said, will disappear
Anyway it'll be invisible soon
Exchanging places with stars now in my head
To be growing rice in China through the night.

Magnetic storms across the solar plains
Make Aurora Borealis shimmy bright
Beyond the mountains to the north.

Closing the lookout in the morning
Thick ice on the shutters
Coyotes almost whistling on a nearby ridge
The mountain is THERE (between two lakes)
I brought back a piece of its rock
Heavy dark-honey color
With a seam of crystal, some of the quartz
Stained by its matrix
Practically indestructible
A shift from opacity to brilliance
(The Zenbos say, "Lightning-flash & flint-spark")
Like the mountains where it was made

What we see of the world is the mind's
Invention and the mind
Though stained by it, becoming
Rivers, sun, mule-dung, flies—
Can shift instantly
A dirty bird in a square time

Gone
Gone
REALLY gone
Into the cool
O MAMA!

Like they say, "Four times up,
Three times down." I'm still on the mountain.

Sourdough Mountain 15:VIII:55
Berkeley 27–28:VIII:56

NOTE: The quotes of Empedocles and Heraclitus are from John
Burnet, *Early Greek Philosophy* (Meridian Books, New York).

Metaphysical Insomnia Jazz.
Mumonkan XXIX.

                                            Of
Course I could go to sleep right here
With all the lights on & the radio going

(April is behind the refrigerator)

              Far from the wicked city
              Far from the virtuous town
              I met my fragile Kitty
              In her greeny silken gown
fairly near the summit of Nanga Parbat & back again, the
              wind flapping the prayer-flags

"IT IS THE WIND MOVING."
_____

"IT IS THE FLAG MOVING."

Hypnotized by the windshield swipes, Mr. Harold Wood:
              "Back & forth;   back & forth."

              We walked beside the moony lake
              Eating dried apricots
              Lemons bananas & bright wedding cake
              & benefits forgot
              _____

"IT IS THE MIND MOVING."
_____

& now I'm in my bed alone
Wide awake as any stone

                                            7:IV:58

HYMNUS AD PATREM SINENSIS

I praise those ancient Chinamen
Who left me a few words,
Usually a pointless joke or a silly question
A line of poetry drunkenly scrawled on the margin
        of a quick splashed picture – bug, leaf,
            cariacature of Teacher –
On paper held together now by little more than ink
& their own strength brushed momentarily over it

Their world and several others since
Gone to hell in a handbasket, they knew it –
Cheered as it whizzed by –
& conked out among the busted spring rain cherryblossom winejars
Happy to have saved us all.

31 : VIII : 58

I Think of Mountains

I keep thinking of Matlock Lake, nobody can live there
Not for long, it's Government land over two miles high
Not enough air (which gives you notions,
    "This is real, this is true")
University Peak stands/falls just overhead, the mistaken idea
"Of mountains he is Sumeru," a little over 13000 feet

Wednesday morning's "test-shot" from Nevada, I figured
"The mountain has split, the Goddess has appeared!"

They've had these thoughts in India thousands of years
& every minute millions die of them—
Radiation sickness from the mountains

It is only a question of balance—
Power and knowledge their proper economy
Are we stuck at last with Aristotle?

When I came down to Berkeley my cottage was a birdhouse
I had to crawl in the door on my hands and knees I was
    immense!
What was I doing there? What was the ceiling for? The walls?

        I NO LONGER HAD TO BREATHE

Nobody could live there, town of perpetual childhood
Babyland the wrong door of the time-machine
No changes except the buildings and trees no future
Except Five o'clock or the week-end about to happen
        (Life stops at midnight Sunday)

To DO anything (consciously) NOW
A problem, paradox, quandary.
The disciples, the hearers listen in silence
The inside boys don't crack a smile
The Big Wheel hollers "Turtle eggs!"

The difference between wisdom and ignorance
The potential between them
A current of human misery (freedom and slavery) which
Can be accurately measured

The mountain a lump of granite in my skull
My mouth filled with Indian corpse meat

28:X:58

"Awake a moment"

Awake a moment
Mind dreams again
Red roses black-edged petals

8:V:59

Haiku, for Gary Snyder

                    IS
Here's a dragonfly
            (TOTALLY)
Where it was,

        that place no longer exists.

15:I:60

A Vision of the Bodhisattvas

They pass before me one by one riding on animals
"What are you waiting for," they want to know

Z—, young as he is (& mad into the bargain) tells me
"Some day you'll drop everything & become
        a *rishi*, you know."

I know
The forest is there, I've lived in it
        more certainly than this town? Irrelevant—

        What am I waiting for?
A change in customs that will take 1000 years to come about?
Who's to make the change but me?

                "Returning again and again," Amida says

Why's that dream so necessary? walking out of whatever house
alone
Nothing but the clothes on my back, money or no
Down the road to the next place the highway leading to the
mountains
From which I absolutely must come back

What business have I to do that?
I know the world and I love it too much and it
Is not the one I'd find outside this door.

                                31:III:60

Philippic, Against Whitehead and a Friend

Pull it down over our faces and ears
That English wool Plato Alfred North Whitehead
And say "there.
The sweater eternally becomes immortal."

I scream HERESY! It's that old slow & gradual salvation
                                                    routine
They tell me "The limits
You must know what are your limitations
And then proceed..."

       (LIMITS: i.e. polite categories & hierarchies
       that justify repression
       "for our own good")

HERESY! Whether its creeping Fabian socialists or that
"Infallible" process you call reality, glued to time so that
      "Justice is later
      Freedom is later
      Dessert comes AFTER the nasty spinach"

     BAH!

I can't help feeling this world is immortality:
Two pigeons in the sun (house cornice across the street)

And nonsense as well! Words, a grammatical order
The world palpably NOT of this order
Exceeds our limits

We kill each other quite artistically
Exquisite tortures, exorbitant crimes

Think of the glass flowers in Peabody Museum
I am limited insofar as huge areas of my brain
Dissolved in Hitler soap-vats
Dispersed as radiant poison over Japan

One of the pigeons flew away the other
Peers down from the cornice
                    Goodies below?
I look up and it's gone, end of the world
        ("invalid argument," Whitehead says, "depending on
        ignorance of the theory of infinite convergent numerical
        series")

Which puts me in over my head

Cantor discovered three orders of infinity:
Aleph-sub-three has yet to be discovered.
I don't consent, I demand the excessive "tertium quid"
That "somewhat" forbidden by Aristotle
That ocean
                (although I'd drown in a pisspot quite as easily)
                (and perhaps my dissent, my perversity, are also
                ruled, have their determined order?)

For limits let's try Blake's
            "Enough—or too much!"
Certainly excesses are deplorable
Those glass flowers at Harvard offensive as the war
I feel better knowing that the secret of their manufacture
Is lost. I'm delighted that the young believe professors
who tell them, *"Ulysses* and *Finnegans Wake* are no-good
failures; Proust killed the novel once and for all."
Whitehead says—and you, my friend!—repeat it:
                "God is the organ of novelty."
I hear an electric organ

Producing pure notes, tone reduced to
    bare vibrational frequency
                (no Pythagorean overtones here,
                Plato his Ideas exactly)
Total purity
Sexless
Absolutely reasonable
Accurately in tune past hell's freezing over
    (within reasonable limits,
        variation due only to line-load and distance from the
        powerhouse)
Precisely and completely what we want
The triumph of the West

Arnold Toynbee tells us this is the true goal of mankind;
Anybody who doesn't want this is uncivilized, out of history.
The psychiatrists tell us if we don't want this we're mad
The government tells us if we don't want this we're goddam
    Communists, GO TO JAIL!

God is worthless except he become a man
Man is a murdering slob unless he exceed himself

The limits,
Orders of infinity:
My own immediate incarnation as compassion and knowledge
Appearing to you
                (who are the ground wherein this manifestation
                proceeds)
                RIGHT NOW!
In response to your necessity
Even though it is I who am deluded
And you who are the Buddhas of this world.

8:V:61

Song to Begin Rōhatsu

Overcome with frustration I sing a few songs
Ring a few bells & wish for better times.
A dim and moisture afternoon.

      FIXED? The race
    is absolutely honest. Very
                straight; OEDIPUS UN-
BOUND.
    the same fate, no matter what his
position relative to an imaginary horizontal plane
          DARUMA
    was there any change.

30:XI:62

Winter Jelly

Now great winter falls
New Year's full moon blur window fog

Words in books drop slowly over brainwheel paddles
        which stand
Clear white ice moon sparkle

28:XII:63

The Lotus Sutra, Naturalized

I got drunk your house
You put that diamond my shirt pocket
How am I supposed to know?
Laying there in drunk tank
            strange town don't nobody know
Get out of jail at last you say
"You already spend that diamond?"
How am I going to know?

27:III:64

Japanese Tea Garden Golden Gate Park in Spring

1.
I come to look at the cherryblossoms
for the last time

2.
Look up through flower branching Deva world
(happy ignorance)

3.
These blossoms will be gone in a week
I'll be gone long before.

That is to say, the cherry trees will blossom every year but I'll disappear for good, one of these days. There. That's all about the absolute permanence of the most impossibly fragile delicate and fleeting objects. By objects, I mean this man who is writing this, the stars, baked ham, as well as the cherryblossoms. This doesn't explain anything.

2:IV:65

Mahayana

Soap cleans itself the way ice does,
Both disappear in the process.
The questions of "Whence" & "Whither" have no validity here.

Mud is a mixture of earth and water
Imagine WATER as an "Heavenly" element
Samsara and nirvana are one:

Flies in amber, sand in the soap
Dirt and red algae in the ice
Fare thee well, how very delightful to see you here again!

5:IV:65

TARA

This bronze Tara this bronze lady
Represents that Lady of Heaven I now invoke,
That idea of wisdom that saves more than itself or me
All the universes,

Enlighten us! We murder each other in this night our eyes
              won't tell us anything but fear
All the universes all the probability tracks

.

                    IMMEDIATELY

Her hands form the mudra "Teaching the Law"
Explaining herself.
She also appears as a song, a diagram,
As a pile of metal images in the market, Katmandu
We seldom treat ourselves right.

  ZENSHIN RYUFU
        Philip Whalen

                                    5:IX:65

White River Ode

White River, because white sand
Rotting white granite, fine gravel
Which becomes formal gardens
A truckload of the stuff costs a fortune
Zen temples, embarrassingly rich
Buy lots of it:
> Ryōanji everybody knows—
> Nanzenji's "tiger leap"—Ginkakuji model of Mt. Fuji,
> > waves on "Western Lake"
> White sand oblivion life green stripe death at Ōbai-in
> Foggy tarn of heaven Daitokuji Hōjō
All of it rotted stone from Hieizan
Melted in the Shirakawa (an emperor took that for his name)
> a wide street leading to the mountains

> 2.

I asked the robe I wore
How do you like being home?
White River; mapletree wind
Shirakawa has banks of hewn stone
Wild wisteria blossoms over the water.
Boiled in the bath until I'm high
Purple stonewall flower cascade across the river
White waters yellow tonight—
I'm ashamed to say you'd be no better off in America
Rubber-tired boxed-in river just like home.
> (As long as the moon keeps wiggling
> I know I'm still pouring into my *sake* cup.)
I do this on purpose: moon river dream garden wine

Consciously imitating the saints
     Li Po, Po Chü-I, Tu Fu, Su Tung-p'o
Believing and not believing it all.
Sitting in the night garden
I realize Shirakawa!
Bashō and Murasaki, Seami and Buson
All used to live in this town
(And now the *sake* pot is warm, White River
Flows in one ear and out the other)
Streetcar swings over the canal where
Expecting to see the moon I saw a star.
I sat a few minutes on the porch of Eikan-dō
The temple flows with the stream (what do I wait for?)
Police box, *benjo* and spring moon all mirrored in canal,
I borrow a garden light; the neon hotel
     shines tenderly in the water
Bridge of the Tomb.
I return to the house (a paper lantern)
I hear one singing a Nō song as he walks beside the river
O Kyōto you're still a winner! Four pairs of lovers, two
singers
       and only half a moon—what'll you be like
          in your prime?

   3.
White River falls and rises from the sea
A glacier on Mt. Hood, a river at Government Camp
Creamy thick with stone flour
Outside Tyghe Valley it's clear
A trout stream that my father fished several times a year
Mother found lumps of agate on the gravelly shore
Alder, willow, bracken, tarry pines

My sister and I caught crawdads
Icy water cooling beer and melons
          (O Shirakawa, the Kamo River is a god
          Its waters magically turning red and green)
I thought "We'll all stay here forever," but we went home.
Now here's Kyōto Shirakawa the white river again
Flows out of my skull, white sandy ashes of my parents
Water ouzel, dragonfly, crawfish
Blazing trout and bright carnelian jewels
Never so near, never so far from home.

1:V:66
23:VI:66

Above the Shrine

I found what I didn't expect to find,
    great stone stairway leads to
Vacant lot hilltop where the wind blows and I can see
                  the mountains
    Rocks & weeds & tin cans: anything historical has
    long been gone
Just dirt again, flowering bushes, dwarf bamboo.
There might have been a grand palace here, imperial villa
Boy with a pair of beautiful Manchu lion dogs now

13:VII:66

The War Poem for Diane di Prima

I.
The War as a Manifestation of Destiny. Whose?

I thought of myself as happily sitting someplace quietly
Reading—but now is multiple
Images of people and cars, through lens-cut flowers
    of glass fruit dish
Many more worlds.

I would be sitting quietly reading
The 4th platoon helicopter marines firing into the bushes
    up ahead
Blue and white triangular flags all flap at the same rate,
Esso station across the street (Shirakawa-dori)
Eastern States Standard Oil here we all are,
Asiatically Yours,
Mah-jong on deck of aircraft carrier, Gulf of Tonkin
               remember the Coral Sea

I write from a coffee shop in conquered territory
I occupy, they call me *"he-na gai-jin,"* goofy-looking foreigner
I am a winner.
The postage stamps read NIPPON, the newspaper is dated
          41 SHŌWA   7 MOON   16 SUN
(This is the 41st year of the reign SHŌWA of that Divine
Emperor, Holy Offspring of the Sun Goddess)
I am a winner, the signs in the streets
Carefully written in English:
          YANKEE, GO HOME

The radio plays selections from OKLAHOMA
The bookstore tries to sell me new British book about
Aforementioned Holy Infant of *Amaterasu-No-*
Ō-Kamisama
All I wanted was something translated by R. H. Blyth,
18,000 pounds of napalm and a helicopter,
Why do I keep losing the war? Misplacing it?

The Secretary of State came to town
I wasn't invited to meet him.
The Secretary of Agriculture, the Secretary of Labor,
All nice people doing their jobs, quieting the locals
Answering embarrassing questions:
     e.g. *Question.* "What is the Republic of China?"
          Answer. "The Republic of China is a medium-sized
          island, south of Japan. Portuguese navigators
          discovered it 300 years ago. They called it
          Formosa. As for Cochin China, now known as
          Viet Nam, we are now doing all in our power to
          prevent &c. &c."
          Question. "Why?"
          Answer. "Because we can."

I like to think of myself sitting in some cool place
(It's un-Godly hot here, as they used to say)
Reading Mallarmé: *Le vierge, le vivace et le bel aujourd'hui*

Kyōto, *la cité toute proustienne:* Portland when I was young
Katsura River at Arashiyama is The Oaks on the Willamette
Roamer's Rest on the Tualitin, Lake Oswego.
The clouds conceal Miyako, the Hozu becomes a tidal river
The Kyōto smog hides a flat Oregon beach and the Pacific,
    just beyond

Where is home,

> *"Pale hands...*
> *...Beside the Shalimar..."*

Caucasoid, go back to those mountains
Your father is chained there, that rock tilted
Into Chaos, heaved up icy pinnacles and snowy peaks

Astrakhan on the north
Persia on the south
Caspian Sea on the east
Black Sea to the west

From the mouth of the Volga you cross the lake and follow
The Amur River into the Pamir,
Coast along the Black Sea with Medea "in one bark convey'd"
To Athens, Rome, or across the great plateaus and
    Hindu Kush
To Alexandria-in-the-Mountains,
> *"Pale hands...*
> *...agonized them in*
> *farewell ..."*

Among waterlilies where the Arabs killed Buddha
Tara surged out of that gorgeous blooming tank
Gazelle eyes. moon breasts
Pomegranate cheeks, ivory neck
Navel a deep wine-cup
         Moon lady
             Mother of the Sun
Jewel flower music
       APPEARING

There's no question of going or staying
A home or a wandering
                    Here we are

    II.
The Real War.

I sit on the shelf outside my door
Water drops down the rain-chain
Some flies outward instead of continuing link by link

    IGNORANCE   The small
    ACTIVITY   rockpile
    CONSCIOUSNESS   anchors
    NAME & FORM   bottom of the
    SENSE ORGANS   chain also
    CONTACT   harbors a couple
    PERCEPTION   shoots of dwarf
    DESIRE   bamboo, chief
    BEING   weed afflicting
    BIRTH   gardens hereabouts
    ATTACHMENT
    OLD AGE & DEATH
                       *

ÇA IRA,

ça ira!

as the French Revolution goes on teaching us
as the Bolsheviki demonstrated
as that Jesus who keeps bursting from the tomb
("Safe as the Bank of England," people used to say)
        several thousand miles and centuries
        beyond Caesar his gold, the Civil Service

The Seal on the dollar bill still reads,
> *NOVUS ORDO SAECULORUM*
>> a sentiment worth at least four-bits
I want THAT revolution to succeed (1776, USA)
The Russians gave up too soon—
The Chinese keep trying but haven't made it yet

POWER,
anyone?
"Grab it & use it to do GOOD;
Otherwise, Evil Men will, &c &c."
Power of that kind, crude hammers, levers
OUT OF STYLE!
The real handle is a wheel, a foot-pedal, an electric switch
NO MOVING PARTS AT ALL
A CHANGE OF STATE

The war is only temporary, the revolution is
Immediate change in vision
Only imagination can make it work.
No more war poems today. Turn off the general alarm.

III.
The War. The Empire.

When the Goths came into Rome
They feared the Senators were gods
Old men, each resolutely throned at his own house door.
When they finally come to Akron, Des Moines, White Plains,
The nomads will laugh as they dismember us.
Other nations watching will applaud.

There'll be no indifferent eye, nary a disinterested ear.
We'll screech and cry.

A friend tells me I'm wrong,
"All the money, all the power's in New York."
If it were only a matter of money, I'd agree
But the power's gone somewhere else...

(Gone from England, the English now arise
Painters and singers and poets leap from Imperial tombs
Vast spirit powers emanate from Beatle hair)

Powerful I watch the shadow of leaves
Moving over nine varieties of moss and lichen
Multitudes of dragonflies (all colors) the celebrated
Uguisu bird, and black butterfly: wing with trailing edge of
        red brocade
(Under-kimono shown on purpose, as in *Book of Songs*)

I sail out of my head, incandescent meditations
Unknown reaches of clinical madness, I flow into crystal
        world of gems, jewels
Enlightened by granite pine lake sky nowhere movies of Judy
Canova

I'll return to America one of these days
I refuse to leave it to slobs and boobies
I'll have it all back, I won't let it go

Here the locust tree its leaves
Sharp oval flat
I haven't lived with you for over twenty years
Great clusters of white blossom
Leaf perfumed also
Lovely to meet again, far away from home
        (the tree-peony too elegant,

Not to be mentioned, a caress, jade flesh bloom)

My rooms are illuminated by
Oranges and lemons in a bowl,
Power of light and vision: I'll see a way...

Nobody wants the war only the money
fights on, alone.

31:V:66–25:VIII:66

Ushi Matsuri

The Immortals are on the loose again!
One rides a black bull round and round Kōryūji
One reads from a great law scroll
All the others dance and chant

Swollen moon-face Good Luck
Balloon-head blue-eyes Longevity
Suddenly zip into the temple out of sight

>   Bats
>   Tigers
>   Cranes

16:X:66

Success Is Failure

They said, "Po Chü-I, go home"
They couldn't pronounce his name,
They said, "Go home, Hakurakuten!"
You're too exciting, too distracting
We love you too much, go home to China

"The moon," they said,
"The moon's Japanese."

Po Chü-I was never here; he never came to Kyōto.

31:X:66

The Dharma Youth League

I went to visit several thousand gold buddhas
They sat there all through the war,—
They didn't appear just now because I happened to be
          in town
Sat there six hundred years. Failures.
Does Buddha fail. Do I.
Some day I guess I'll never learn.

28:XII:66

Grace Before Meat

You food, you animal plants
I take you, now, I make you wise
Beautiful and great with joy
Enlightenment for all sentient beings
All the hungry spirits, gods and buddhas who are sad

30:V:67

Walking beside the Kamogawa,
Remembering Nansen and Fudō
and Gary's Poem

Here are two half-grown black cats perched on a
          lump of old teakettle brick plastic garbage
               ten feet from the west bank of the River.
I won't save them. Right here Gary sat with dying Nansen,
The broken cat, warped and sick every day of its life,
Puke & drool on the *tatami* for Gary to wipe up & scold,
"If you get any worse I'm going to have you put away!"
The vet injected an overdose of nemby and for half an hour
Nansen was comfortable.

How can we do this, how can we live and die?
How does anybody choose for somebody else.
How dare we appear in this Hell-mouth weeping tears,
Busting our heads in ten fragments making vows &
          promises?

Suzuki Rōshi said, "If I die, it's all right. If I should
live, it's all right. Sun-face Buddha, Moon-face Buddha."
Why do I always fall for that old line?

We don't treat each other any better. When will I
Stop writing it down.

                                        Kyōto 14:IV:69

POSTSCRIPT, 17:IV:69 (from De Visser, Vol. I, pages 197–198), 20th
Commandment of the *Brahmajala Sutra* (Nanjō 1087): "...always
practise liberation of living beings

          (*hō jō,* 放生)"

Tassajara

What I hear is not only water but stones
No, no, it is only compressed air flapping my eardrums
My brains gushing brown between green rocks all
That I hear is me and silence
The air transparent golden light (by Vermeer of Delft)
Sun shines on the mountain peak which pokes
The sun also ablaze &c.
Willard Gibbs, Hans Bethe, what's the answer
A lost mass (Paris gone)
Shine red in young swallow's mouth
Takagamine Road

The water suffers
Broken on rocks worn down by water
Wreck of THE DIVINE MIND on the reef called Norman's Woe
"Suddenly, ignorance," the *Shastra* says.
Moon arises in my big round head
Shines out of my small blue eyes
Tony Patchell hollers "Get it! Get it!"
All my treasure buried under Goodwin Sands

20:VII–25:XI:72

Kitchen Practice

They got it all fixed up the way
They wanted and now
They've changed it back again
They've eaten all the sugar
They've taken all the teapots to their rooms

23:VII:73

The Sesshin Epigram

The hand foresees what the eye
Cannot foretell

8–9:VIII: 73

Zenshinji

Here our days are nameless time all misnumbered
Right where Mr. Yeats wanted so much to be
Moving to the call of bell and semantron,
     rites and ceremonies
Bright hard-colored tidiness Arthur Rackham world
     (no soil or mulch or mud)
Everything boiled and laundered and dry-cleaned
And probably inhabited by that race of
     scrubbed and polished men
     who drive the dairy trucks of San Francisco

The arts ooze forth from fractures in planes of solid rock
Outer ambition and inwards tyranny
"Hurrah for Karamazov!"
Totally insane sprung loose from all moorings
I wander about, cup of coffee in hand,
Chatting with students working in warm spring rain

                                        25:III:74

Somebody Else's Problem Bothers Me

Warm sun and chilly air, water is low and the creek is
    clear
Will I accidentally drop a jade ring in the creek
All the new stones glaring light and airplanes
Shall I drop my gold crown in the pool?
Have I derailed my train of thought?
A rock with an elephant's forehead!
Silver turquoise ring dropped into monk's kimono sleeve
What can we answer?

Yellow tin chimneys.

White-crowned sparrows.

Everything a-tilt.

26:III:76

"Back to Normalcy"

My ear stretches out across limitless space and time
To meet the fly's feet coming to walk on it
The cat opens an eye and shuts it
That much meaning, use or significance

Wind chime, hawk's cry
Pounding metal generator
Bell and board rehearsing bluejays
Dana, phoning, shouts "You mean fiberglass?"
Telephone grapeleaves shake together
Dull blond sycamore sunshine
Dana says, "All you guys bliss out
Behind the carrot and raisin salad?"
Brown dumb leaves fall on bright ferns
New and thick since the fire.

Tassajara, 8–11:XI:77

Discriminations

Earliest morning hot moonlight
A catastrophe, the garden too theatrical
Feels wild, unearthly
H. P. Lovecraft could use his favorite adjective:
"Eldritch"

The "shooting-star" flowers that Mama used to call "bird-bills"
Bloom around the Hogback graveyard
Suzuki Rōshi's great seamless monument
Wild cyclamen, actually, as in the *Palatine Anthology*
I go home to mend my *rakusu* with golden thread.

Tassajara, 24:II:78

What's New?

We keep forgetting the world is alive
Being the same as we
The coathanger and kimono leap off the rail
Hurl themselves to the floor

Instead of the usual instant anger
I pause to admire this prodigy of nature
The kimono flowing in strange billows and festoons
Falling timelessly (if I say so) to the closet floor.

A couple weeks later I'm flailing about
The rug rippled and ruched, table cockeyed
Something tips over, I (furious) grab, rush,
Breathless dark living room
Why can't you, what's to stop your doing
Whatever you want to do—collect SOMETHING
Fill in the blanks later, unexpected brilliant excursions
And back again to the central trunk or channel

Watching the "waterfall" (more accurately, "water curtain")
In Beale St. PGE has done something to my head
I see myself, all persons, animals, trees &c
FALLING through space, dividing and disintegrating
Halfway down, some are shattered on the first step of the "fall"
Fragments thrown into the narrow pool next below "inevitably"
And then pumped, I suppose, to some tank or pool
      (roof garden?)
Above.

I like to think there's a garden and pond,
Plain green shrubs, maybe azaleas or camellias in tubs
Doors from the company restaurant open onto it
The pond a formal baroque design as at
    Inoda Coffee Shop in Kyōto
White smooth concrete framing it, mechanical but pleasing
("Grooming displacement behavior"?)

After murdering Kesa Gozen—by his own mistake
But her design—Endō Morito stood under the waterfall
Three weeks in a row, invoking Fudō Myō-ō
And came out as Mongaku Shonin the famous monk
Who went really crazy with political intrigue
Lost everything at last and died in exile,
Sado Island, 1193.

4, 27:XII:78

Welcome Back to the Monastery

A wildly crowded noisy breakfast
Sixty people sounding like 7500 in the highschool
gymnasium
A small town in Arkansas where the people haven't
    seen each other
In a long time
> "Just lucky enough to have thought about bringing
> this little bit of lunch with us—few scraps of fried
> chicken, 3 or 4 pounds of potato salad, salami sand-
> wiches, potato chips, dill pickles and some chocolate
> chip cookies, in case the dinner was late or they
> wasn't anything planned..."

I wished for nasturtium seeds
They appear spontaneously *via* interoffice mail
Neurotic smoke alarm gibbers in the zendō
Its batteries going stale
Every morning cold air on my shaved head
Wakes me before the alarm clock
Can you hear the echo? Do you see the reflection?

Tassajara, 13–15:I:79

The Bay Trees Were About to Bloom

For each of us there is a place
Wherein we will tolerate no disorder.
We habitually clean and reorder it,
But we allow many other surfaces and regions
To grow dusty, rank and wild.

So I walk as far as a clump of bay trees
Beside the creek's milky sunshine
To hunt for words under the stones
Blessing the demons also that they may be freed
From Hell and demonic being
As I might be a cop, "Awright, move it along, folks,
It's all over, now, nothing more to see, just keep
Moving right along"

I can move along also
"Bring your little self and come on"
What I wanted to see was a section of creek
Where the west bank is a smooth basalt cliff
Huge tilted slab sticking out of the mountain
Rocks on the opposite side channel all the water
Which moves fast, not more than a foot deep,
Without sloshing or foaming.

Tassajara, 11:II:79

Treading Water. Backing & Filling.

Here beyond the Hogback I fling myself into the creek
Water not quite chest high, cold and fast
I let the breeze dry me and all of you on this page
Written in the sun where big spiders play on the rocks
Big black butterfly with cream edged wings investigates
What is the justice of any claim? Which Real,
    which "allowable"?
What I want is to get loose; not to claim or be claimed,
Falling elegantly over the rocks into the creek and gone
Silent, living, moving; sometimes roar, bubble, splash
White, clear, dark smooth, move.
I said once before, "Wet is comfort."
Probably I'm too fishy to be a seagull;
More likely a walrus or sealion.

Here is one specific contentment: shade beside a rapids
A little fall cascading down the opposite rocky bank
Fountains of the Boboli Gardens I doubt that I'll ever visit.
This leaves all Italian gardens wonderful imaginary elegance:
What the designer imagined but didn't get.

How to explain that everything is unimaginably splendid
And horrible? Or that my life at this moment is enormously
Satisfying and dreadful?
Who can resist replying, "So what else is new you got flowers
In the ass?" (O Spring, &c &c!)
& I, "Why ain't you glad I should be feeling wonderful?"
& you, exasperated, "NATURALLY you're happy—you are
    heartless
And haven't a single brain in your head!"

I grow fatter and fatter and fatter, like the ox who wanted
To be a frog. He bought a tight green suit and went to sit
On a lilypad. One croak and the buttons flew off; two croaks
And the trousers burst; three croaks and the lilypad sank
The whole project a failure

What does the naked man say. Hot and cold, wet and dry,
　　　rough and smooth.
Things are variously colored but that seems an impertinent
Fact. The wind is warm and dry. Lots of my skin
Is still wet.

The shadow of the naked man says, "You are too fat, even
　　　if you
Stand with both hands on top of your head." The shadow of a
Young man with a round head and big ears; it doesn't know
How old it is.

In order to be calm and mellow
One must take time to find out what it is and practice it
So that when the atmosphere becomes busy and buggy,
　　　Everybody rushing about,
Seeking who to blame for the confusion
They are so industriously creating....
Calm mellowness may not be necessary to me
But will be there for other folks to enjoy—supposing anybody
In all the world is interested in these commodities.
The noisy creek reminds me of silk weaving looms in Kyōto.

Tassajara, 6–7:III:79

And Then...

Everything else begins or stops
Talking into sleepy ears of night
Coals far down are bright red universe of another size
Only a few square inches but still hot as ever, all connected
All perfectly understandable, all night. Go home by moonlight.
Beyond that the molecules divide it up among themselves.
Whether we walk or stand still, very tiny threads provide us
With news of moonlight or we are paralyzed and forget
The multiplication table.

When they are awake they don't remember
        having listened all night.
Do you follow my drift (I think all that part is about
A gold mine)
A veritable treasure underground
Out to lunch, off the wall, down the tubes
The sun is in Chicago.

Tassajara, 29 or 30:IV:79

The Ghosts

Of people dead fifty years and not only people—
Theaters and streetcars and large hotels follow me
Into this dusty little gully. None of them ever liked California
Why don't they stay in Portland where they belong.
I'm tired of them.

A new ghost in this morning's dream,
Beautiful and young and still alive
How far will that one follow me? I'm not chasing any,
Any more.

Tassajara, 14:VII:79

Hot Springs Infernal in the Human Beast

Examine a big stone across the creek
    outside the kitchen window
Instead of walking out to coffee? Saved by the real world
    again!
Walk.
Get away from here? Go read thermometer in the garden;
Fingernails unaccountably dirty.

        hummingbird

I gross and unwieldy, torpid and silent
I must begin to flap new plumes, great wings
And sing a one-eyed song of Halicarnassus in the spring
Old and immense and hastening to die
Clutch wildly at any spark of life

        hummingbird

Yellow anemone
Purple morning Glory
Four nasturtiums (ORANGE)

Tassajara, 5:X:79

Homage to Hart Crane

As golden yellow as possible
The rocks blue-green as T'ang Dynasty
Clothing colors mudded out—red, yellow, blue, green, black
Animals, imaginary lions, elephants and tigers
Realistic birds. I need a big collection of Crayolas.

Image flowers in mirror landscape sexier
Under glass, poem or picture
Reflection statuary reflecting lights and images
Are there many places.
Only by looking at small details of moss or flower centers
Through a magnifying glass

"uncathected Oedipal backlash; schizoid mirror worlds of
     brilliant silence"

Now I find I've skipped all carelessly onto this page
Leaving the opening preceding this one blank
Fetch the colors! Summon the genius!

Restriction of the view by round window frame
Lends something of the thick
Unobtainable silence of mirrors
When looking at a distant landscape from a great height
Something of the same feeling occurs
The part of the world "over there," mountains &c
Is absolutely silent

While the place where one stands is nearly still.
Hell yes.
A distinct blue line. The thread of the discourse
Tightens up too much; puckers the fabric.

Tassajara, 23–26:X:79

Preface from Heavy Breathing

The most interesting thing about this book is that it was written under ideal conditions. The author was living a life of elegant retirement in the character of a Zen Buddhist priest at the Hossen Temple in San Francisco and at the monastery of Zenshinji at Tassajara Springs, far in the mountains east of Big Sur. Given ideal conditions, how could life be anything but a joyous round of pleasure. What could possibly go wrong.

At the top of the hill above the Third Culvert (counting from the first one over Cabarga Creek as one ascends the road to and from Tassajara) I sat down for a minute to consider what's possible. A sentence, a word, a monkey flower. Sun heats, wind cools, simultaneously. What am I after. From this point the road is uphill and downhill. The flowers are too pale to be monkey flowers. They aren't the exact color of wild azaleas. My ears fry in the sunlight. There are monkey flowers no matter what I say, just as K. M. still has a terrible cough this morning. Wild larkspurs have three different shades of blue.

Early the next morning I find that my brains have come loose and are floating up against the skull bones, gently bumping and knocking with the motions of the tide. I used to believe that I could do anything so long as I really understood that there'd be consequences, whether pleasant or unpleasant, consequences of specific size, shape, color and duration. They were to be accepted and digested. (People used to say, "Never buy anything you can't eat.") Now I'm uncertain whether all the consequences of any—even the simplest—action can be known immediately; I fear that some of the smaller details which one may have overlooked may bring about a disaster which will arrive at the door on some innocently beautiful Sunday morning. Why not.

At the turnout above the Third Culvert I found a set of *juzu* beads which I hadn't realized leaving or losing. There they were drying in the sun beside variegated lupine flowers. At sundown that day I noted that a great wind was blowing lumps and sheets of cloud across the narrow sky; maybe that's all that was scheduled to happen that day. Later the air was fresh and still. The full moon appeared.

Returned to the city after many months I find too many things in my rooms and not enough air. What can be is a slice of Nob Hill in the distance. Radio delivers KJAZ without hesitation. No ideas or anything; imported beer. There was a visit to the rhododendrons blooming in the Park. In Stockton Street, Gregory Corso hollers to me from the window of his mother-in-law's blue station wagon, also blooming. (Max doesn't say hello but appears and disappears, grinning, from under an Army blanket on the floor of the car behind his father's seat.) Ideal conditions prevail in the city and in the country. I continue, after all; and the consequences.

Tassajara/San Francisco, 1980

Epigrams & Imitations

I
ACTIONS OF BUDDHA

Clip cuticle; drink orange juice
"be confirmed by 10,000 things"
(the next line after that is delinquent)
   turtles

II
UPON THE POET'S PHOTOGRAPH

This printed face doesn't see
A curious looking in;
Big map of nothing.

III
FROM THE JAPANESE OF KAKINOMOTO HITOMARO

What though my shorts are threadbare
I deserve all your love

IV
FALSE *SENRYŪ*

A cough
waits for the bus.

V
PERPETUUM MOBILE

Everybody has a car
But something's wrong with it

We are going very fast—
Have you noticed
The driver is a headless corpse

VI
THE CONCEALED PHOENIX
TREASURE JEWEL TERRACE,
AFTER LI HO

Mountains dream tigers and monkeys
The sea imagines dragons
Monstrous birds trouble the air.
The moon bothers all & sundry,
with or without reflection.

1981

Dharmakaya

The real thing is always an imitation
Consider new plum blossoms behind the zendō

20:I:81

"Silence in the middle of traffic"

Silence in the middle of traffic
Men's heads explode in Beirut
Men's hearts explode in the zendō
Who's going to pick up the pieces?
Your finger's on the detonator button.

Zenshin, 29:X:83
(last night of 7-day
sesshin, Hosshinji)

At Dharma Sangha

We open the zendō at six p.m.
Sometimes people come.
Here we are stillness parked in silence
Great big nothing happens in imaginary void.

In the morning, old paving blocks tip
    as I circumambulate the chörten
Climbing to Forester Pass, under my boots
Upstairs in the Villa Borghese
Tippy marble floor slab (clank)

26:VII, 3:VIII:86

On the Way to the Zendō

A reverse wind blows freeway sounds up-canyon
    through yellow leaves
Ducks quack and cluck flying to Bosque del Apache
SOME VERSIONS OF THE PASTORAL whistle in one ear,
    out the other.
Christopher Robin, Pooh and Piglet
Stomping through the Hundred Acre Wood.

18:IX:86

22:Ⅶ:82

What Are You Studying, These Days?

The electronic watch runs backwards to five A.M.
At night I read with broken eyes
How to control the Universe: compel
     with mantra, mandala, vision—
Summon, seal, dissolve, bind, subjugate & destroy &c
Powers to do what is already being done anyway
"Power to do good," or "Sufficient unto the day is
     the evil thereof"
"Sweet Analytics, 'tis thou hast ravish'd me"

The Merry-go-round, the Ferris Wheel
The shoot-the-chutes

Your trouble is you're not very real, are you.
Hallucinatory fountain pens, eh?
Skin chips and flaky on the outside
Internal organs all blackened and shriveled
What do you expect with too much in mind
Too busy to see or hear a single particular?
I have put on a gown of power I didn't know I had—
Or wanted.

Tassajara, 20:XI:79